I0418735

RELEASING THE PAST

A BACK-OF-THE-TOILET BOOK
ABOUT HOW TO
REALLY LET SH*T GO

KIMBERLY CLO

Copyright © 2025 Kimberly Clo

The author reserves all rights to be recognized as the owner of this
work. You may not sell or reproduce any part of this book without
written consent from the copyright owner, including internet usage,
without permission from Cielo International Press. Brief quotations
for critical articles and reviews allowed.

First paperback edition April 2025

Cover design by Katherine Petillo
Cover art by Kimberly Clo
Editing by Tim Clo and Shannon Jackson Arnold

Quotes included under the fair use doctrine.

Printed in the United States

ISBN 979-8-9985144-0-1

Published by Cielo International Press, Madison, TN

Cielo International Press is the publishing branch of
Cielo International LLC and House Of Clo Productions

www.KimberlyClo.com

RELEASING THE PAST
A BACK-OF-THE-TOILET BOOK ABOUT
HOW TO REALLY LET SH*T GO

by
KIMBERLY CLO

CIELO INTERNATIONAL
PRESS

Dedication

To my husband Tim Clo, who is a living example of
embodied masculine beauty and mature responsible
care.

My kite string holder, thank you for the consistent
unconditional positive regard you have for me and for
your decision to never shame me for being myself.

Always is as always does.
107

Table Of Contents

By letting it go
it all gets done.
The world is won
by those who let it go.

—Lao Tzu

It's "Go" Time

I hope you're sitting down for this, friend...

We are about to have an important and surprisingly refreshing conversation about life, poop, and one way you may not have thought of to really let shit go.

Sharing my insights on the subject is best delivered in the form of this little book. It will be more comfortable for us both if you have some auditory and olfactory privacy.

We are going to talk about how pooping is a metaphor for letting go of emotional things.

This whole book is really an elaborate *love*-scheme on my part to get you to connect to your body and experience a real shift in the way your Life Force flows, making it easier to make the exchange of letting go of the old to make room for the new.

Our lives, much like our digestive systems, function best when we participate consciously in the robust exchange of the old for the new.

But many of us are out of synch with that repeating cycle. There is often a break in the flow physically and emotionally — if we can find the block (or the leak) we can course-correct and maybe even discover a new way of letting in the new and peacefully letting the rest go.

Yes, I'm talking about poop—but really it's about your life and the past and how to move forward without dragging a bunch of old shit around.

At the end of the day, everyone poops. And if we don't poop we feel like crap and then we die.

There is no way around this.

Not only do our bodies need to poo to let go of food waste — our hearts and minds also have to let go of the past. Past events, past hurts, past mistakes, past relationships, past foot-in-mouth moments you've replayed in your head too many times.

These things happened and we experienced them for what they were — good or bad. Even the positive experiences must go down the hatch — in the same way that the cleanest eating vegan still gets gassy and has to release. No one gets out of it. We are a part of a cycle that is bigger than us.

I started writing this book for myself...

To make my husband laugh, I often say "I'm gonna go release the past" to let him know I'm heading into the loo for a #2. The phrase would "stick" in my head for the duration of my stay. It was funny to me but it also made me think about what it means to *release the past*. At the time I was grappling with some painful experiences that I needed to let go of in order to forgive and heal from my pain.

Holding on to past wrongs, my own included, was poisoning my mind and worse — poisoning my future.

As I sat, I wrote these little *anal*ogies and musings in my Notes app. This went on for several years. Writing it slowly and chock full of poop humor gave the whole depth of what I was navigating some levity which helped the medicine go down. And to be clear, never in a million years did I imagine publishing it! Especially not as a first book! But, alas, it is the book I had been writing all along.

I am not an expert at letting go. But I have had a lot of experience doing it...and *not* doing it.

Holding on is worse.
Letting go is better.

This book is my attempt to share the nourishing goodness that I have digested and used to create a new life for myself.

And now I'm writing this book for you.

You have seen some shit.

You are probably the hero in one person's story and the villain in someone else's. You are complex and perhaps you've already been doing your inner work to "own your shit" and do better next time.

You want a better world. You want better relationships. You want a better experience of being human.

I see you (well, not this actual moment, thank goodness), and while I cannot guarantee that this book will *fully* cause you to experience a better world,
better relationships, and a better experience of being human (only you can do that), this book *does* point in that general direction. And it might illuminate some things that hide where the sun does not ordinarily shine.

This book makes me laugh.
It makes me think.

It makes me happy.

It is my hope that it will do the same for you.

And also — this is "no joke."

For some people, the mechanics of their digestive systems are not moving things out, and it's very serious. As I'm sure you have guessed, I am no doctor. If pooping is a prolonged challenge for you, I recommend seeking out medical support. I have tender empathy for anyone dealing with severe and life-threatening digestive-related illnesses. If this applies to you, I send you so much compassion and empathy as you navigate this painful challenge.

Ways you can use this book

This book is made up of stand-alone bits of writing and you can read it however you wish:

- You can read all at once from end to end if you like. However, I find that some of the passages are quite nutritionally dense and may need some time to digest. Bingeing the whole book at once can be quite a load.
- You can jump in anywhere and enjoy a little nugget on the run.
- You can flip through and snack on just the poetry bits.
- You can take one morsel at a time in whatever way feels the most peaceful to you. This content, while it's bowel-shakingly funny, may be a lot to take in (and let go of) for such a wee book.

Haiku or is it HaiPoo?

Throughout this book I will be peppering you with some haikus I have written over the years inspired by this whole project.

I call them HaiPoos and they are indicated by this little symbol : :

And in case you want to play along at home, I have provided some space and instructions at the back of this book for you to write your own HaiPoos.

This is a weird little book...

written in a funny little way...

about how you can see something very ordinary in a

whole new light.

I hope you enjoy the ride, have a laugh and leave the room a little lighter than when you walked in.

::

For existential

and excremental crisis,

only one way out.

::

Thank you, hard poopie.

You let me know I need to

hydrate and relax.

The NewPoo Review

Just before the big show, when it's "places everybody" backstage, let that be your cue to set an intention for yourself that this will be an "on purpose" poo.

Begin by doing a "Thank You" ride through your body.

Thank your body for processing the food you have eaten and think about all that has happened in your life lately that you don't want to hold any more.

Put one hand on your heart, one on your belly.

Just be with yourself now.

Connect to your heart and mind in these few minutes and send yourself some really genuine gratitude and love.

Experiment with sending purposeful gratefulness to your intestines and your esophagus, send love to your liver,

to your kidneys and bladder,

send smiles and love to your skin and teeth and hair.

Go ahead and get weird about it.

Make it a loving quest to leave no part of yourself un-appreciated.

Tune in now to your heart — can you feel it beating through those miles and miles of arteries and veins?

Send that strong, beating gratitude right to and through your brave heart.

This kind of work is a real challenge and worthy of the effort.

Use this time to let go and fill the void that is being created with generous, full, unconditional love and compassion for all your organs and bones and brains.

Be as present with yourself as much as you can right now.

Review the days or hours since your last poo and tell the body to do a quick sweep of any little emotional dingleberries and soul waste that does not serve and when you open up the hatch, may it all go down the tubes together.

: :

How you do one thing

is how you do everything.

Master dropping it.

: :

When you lean to clean,

if you have the chance,

use that bidet, friend.

The "Analog Poo" Session

Consider leaving those digital devices in the other room and instead go for what I call "an analog poo session" (or is it "*anal* log"?)

This one, small gesture of choosing to go technologically commando is a very real way of showing up for yourself. It's a way of telling your subconscious mind that you're not "messing around."

What you want to release is worth a few moments of focus and attention. Be present with yourself right now. There is a bunch of stuff rearranging inside. It's rumbly. It's on the move — and if you roll with it, it can feel kinda cool.

Be with what it feels like in there.

Feel it and remember the magnificent body you live in and how amazing it is that it has such an effective system of release.

What if our emotions could be processed in the same basic way as our food?

A bunch of stuff is moving around in our guts, feelings and emotions. The subconscious sorts out what is nutrient and what is chaff.

Life is meant to move thru us.

We are not created to carry around the indigestible, toxic, expired thoughts, feelings or emotions of life that were intended to be experienced and then released.

We were not created to carry emotional shit any more than we were intended to carry around literal shit.

When you think about it, that makes it much easier to let old experiences go when we see it in a new way.

Leaving the phone out of the room helps us focus and get clear so we can be with what is real.

"If I'm not on my phone — what am I supposed to do in here?" you might wonder.

As you sit, you make room for whatever your own mind and heart want to say.

You decide what you want to release — say it and acknowledge it one final time in all its inglorious rank.

If you make the decision to really doo this, it can be the very last time you ever review and experience that thing from the past.

And should those habituated thoughts return, you remind yourself that you have already flushed that one and you will not give your mind, your time, or your attention to that experience again.

: :

Sometimes I just cry

when I remember the things

I've carried so long.

: :

That weird fish I ate

last night has left the building.

Good riddance to you.

The Tool Is The Stool

"Who... does... number... 2... work... for?"
— Austin Powers

It's *you*, friend.

Make that number 2 work for you, and let's get the most out of this opportunity.

Take it as seriously or as playfully as you feel like. Poop is funny. Farts are funny. You are funny. You are in charge of your own good time.

You can start by thinking of something you want to release that is easy and not too emotional of a load to begin with. Pick something simple that you never want to think about again and start there.

Maybe it's the guy who cut you off in traffic, or the weird confusing look a co-worker gave you.

Now that you have something in mind to release — imagine that thing as being fully obedient to your will.

19

Imagine now that no matter what you decide to release, everything inside of you from your expired cells and that extra fiber to all the worn-out thoughts and beliefs that you are ready to surrender...will *all* obey your command — you just give the word.

Using your powerful imagination, tell your subconscious mind to send any painful emotions, annoyances and old shit you just don't want to think about for one more second — direct all of that on purpose — to your brave and noble bowels.

Then when you can't or don't want to hold it any more, experience the very real and satisfying feeling of being empty of it all. The perfect poo.

This is the real time to pay attention — don't miss out on feeling the heaviness dropping out the bottom! Let that feeling of release sink in and replace refuse with peace.

I realize it's gross, but honestly, there are few pleasures in life like the release of a full, strong, complete poo (with a tidy paperwork process).

Delight in the whole cycle. You have made a real decision and your body will always comply with your thoughts. That is the only way we ever change.

Like they say . . .

As above, so below.

As within, so without.

If it has meaning in the material world, it has meaning in the immaterial world.

It can be no other way. Hack the system. Make that poo work for you.

::

Is what I consume

in real life consuming me?

Consumed by the past?

::

If it wasn't good,

better have a smart reason

to hold on so tight.

When Things Don't Go According To Plan

Sometimes it's...

Too fast

Too slow

Too painful

Too burny

Too crampy

Maybe it's...

Dry heaves with no pay-off.

Or too wee a turd considering all the time invested.

Sometimes it's been days and days and every time you sit it feels like an unanswered prayer.

It works the same in our minds and hearts when we make efforts to let the past go. Sometimes we are carrying a *load* of...

resistance,

anger,

justification,

resentment,

judgments,

victim mentality,

blame.

It will require some mindful attention in order for them to release.

When you find yourself here you can get curious and ask...

Can I have empathy for what's going on in my inner world?

What does my body need in order to move in the healthiest way?

Do I need a therapist or other support in letting go?

Do I need to be around people more?

Do I need to be around people less?

Is there something inside my heart and mind that I am having trouble letting go of?

Am I giving my attention to things that hurt and were never meant to stay inside?

Am I expecting others to change in order for me to let go?

Whether others change the way you want them to – or if they don't – what they decide will never un-doo the fact that it's YOU who has to release your own past.

No one can poo your poo for you.

: :

There are no saviors.

You gotta take your own shits.

There's no other way.

: :

Sometimes I wonder

what is the best thing I can

eat, drink, hear, see, feel?

What You Feed On Is Feeding On You

As you probably know, micro organisms are a thing.

When we eat our favorite food, delicious though it may be, there are often little bitty fellas living in there, things like parasites, viruses and bacteria.

They are a natural part of life here on Earth.
Bigger things eat littler things and even littler things catch a ride by slipping in under the radar.

According to the robots...

"Parasites obtain their nourishment from their host organism. Depending on the type of parasite, they may feed on:

- *Blood*
- *Tissue*
- *Nutrients from the host's digestive system*

- *Waste products*
- *Cells*

Micro organisms eat dead organisms, animal waste, plant litter, and other organic matter."

- Google

They feed on us

Parasites deplete us of the nutrients we need while they go on reproducing and getting stronger.

Just like those hungry, horny little parasites, something else is feeding on us — it's called the World Wide Web — especially any platform that lets you scroll such as social media, shopping sites, video sharing sites. You can tell what they are up to by the name *they* gave it — it's literally called a "feed".

Your social media feed offers up whatever it knows you can't say "no" to. It offers me whatever it knows I can't resist.

How does it know what we find irresistible?
Because we keep saying "yes" to it.
We keep giving it our attention and our energy.
It will keep offering it up as long as we consume it.

We feed on them

Hours and hours we feed on content.
Some of it is incredibly educational and teaches us, enlightens us, trains us, but the evidence suggests that no matter what you inquire about, the return of information will be inexhaustible. You will get back a fountain of information that is never-ending, even when we want to be done and look away, there is more

and more
and more

offered up to us around every cyber corner we turn. It's enough to choke a horse. It's more information than we could ever possibly take in and it can feel overwhelming even when it's about helpful subjects we are interested in.

A lot of our feed makes us sick and robs us of the soul nutrients we need in order to be healthy humans.

Nutrients like joy,
like connection,
like experimentation,
like creativity.
These are living parts of us and they will shrivel up like a neglected house plant when they don't receive the regular watering of our literal attention and experiential energy.

It's natural to ask, seek, explore. And the Internet is a great place for answers. It's just good to be aware that it's hijacking your curiosity and that's how they get ya.

Ask and it is given. Seek and ye shall find. Knock and the door will be opened. That is how this universe appears to work.

May I be more mindful of what I seek and whom I ask and upon which doors I knock.

You are what you eat

The algorithm knows that we are all unique and its job is to keep our attention so it can scour the web looking for more of what it knows we will consume.

Your personal feed, your AI is curated by *your* personal tastes and interests and thirst traps and the things that can snag your attention reliably.

My feed and AI is filled with *my own* interests, queries, and my kind of thirst traps — the things I find irresistible.

It's easy to believe that the Internet and AI looks the same for everyone, but it doesn't — not even close.

Your feed is an aspect of you.
My feed is an aspect of me.

The internet is the host.
W*e* are the parasite.
We are the virus.

We are the thing that is feeding on the web and the web is feeding on us.

The kicker is — that shit is TASTY!!

It's delicious and it goes down smoothly.

Like eating an off-brand Little Debbie Snack Cake.
That oily coated sugar sponge, void of nutritional value or substance and chock-full of actively horrible toxic preservatives is *exactly* what it feels like to me when I graze at that feeding tube of a phone that dumps its content right into my brains.

Ugh. And yet, knowing all of this, we still do it.
We love the exchange and so does the algorithm.

How can you tell that you are being parasitically consumed by the internet?

You can tell by the shit that comes out of your mouth. The crap you talk about that feeds fear.

The shit you say that sounds word-for-word exactly like the talking points you were feeding on moments ago in your 24-hour news feed.

You can tell it's coming from that source because it causes you to judge others who are different, to act like you aren't safe in moments when you really *are* safe, and to justify actions that isolate you from community and from your own inner source of creation.

When we get all hopped-up on fear, and twitchy about things we can't control, it's time for a cleanse.

I offer an alternative for your consideration:

Feed on and be fed by the natural world.
Everything about nature feeds us.
The soil,
the air,
the sun,
the water,
the vistas,
the moon,
the stars.
It all feeds us and feels *really* good.

Nature is full of *healthy* bacteria and micronutrients.

Our gut has a flourishing microbiome that can, when it's operating in a healthy way, consume and excrete all manner of things we take in.

There is potential for an eternal healthy exchange cycle of feeding and releasing waste on the wee level of the micro-biome.

How do we know that there is a healthy exchange happening?

Because we can see it in things we create on purpose with our hands,
our voices,
our beautiful minds.

When we write and dance and sing, we are offering the healthy fruit of our Being out into the world.

Someone could feed on it and be nourished. They could become stronger, and more loving consuming the good food we offer up.

There is nothing wrong with the fact that there are parasites and viruses in the world. It's natural. And when we are wise, we make simple easy choices based on how reality actually works.

We can wash our lettuce,
we can wash our hands,
we can wash our minds,
we can choose to practice "mind safety" the way we practice "food safety".

By our decision to be mindful and attentive we can be sure that the things we put in our bodies and minds stand a greater chance to nourish us in helpful, creative ways, rather than deplete us of our capacity to create.

I can ask...

"Does this inspire me to create or consume?"

Creation is the name of the game.
We did not come here as human beings simply to be entertained, we came here to create and to experience ourselves as individuals materialized in this 3D world.

You came to create the thing that only YOU can create.
We can create anything from masterpieces to moments.
We can create meals,
friendships,
conversations,
games,
gardens,
songs,
stories,
experiences,
adventures,
babies.
We carve, we knit, we build, we relate, we cry, we connect,
we draw. We have countless ways to create!

You can ask...

Does what I feed upon nourish me so that I can create?

Is my feed *feeding on me* or depleting me of my desire to
create?

Does my feed encourage me to imagine and create a Beautiful Future for myself? My community? My world?

Does my feed discourage me from imagining a Beautiful Future? Does it make me feel hopeless and impotent and afraid?

What You Put In Is What You Get Out

"Smelly cat, smelly cat, what are they feeding you?"
— Phoebe Buffay of Friends

What are you feeding yourself?

What are you feeding your mind?

What are you feeding your ears?

What are you feeding your heart?

What are you feeding your inner child?

What are you feeding your dreams?

What are you feeding your future?

What are you feeding your children?

What are you feeding your partner?

What are you feeding your social media pages?

What are you feeding your co-workers?

What are you feeding your friendships?

What are you feeding your community?

What are you feeding yourself — body, mind and spirit?

Your answer to these questions will help you make sense of the nature and quality of your letting go process. Or not.

: :

I've been here before.

Ten thousand times I have sat.

First time to let go.

: :

Fight the temptation

to polish your turd, my guy.

Own it and let go.

The Long, Slow Drop

There is a mercy and a compassion for the long, slow drop. Some things are just sticky and hard, and we have to be patient with our systems of digestion and forgiveness.

You might be thinking something like, "I really don't want to let it go.... at least the past is familiar and it feels better to me than the fast-moving, unpredictable future we are barreling toward!"

Or you might be thinking, "What if I've had to let so many things go already? I would love to just hold on to something familiar and reliable for once?"

Some things take a really long time to let go. Some things require therapy and modalities and hours of journaling and really deep shadow work.

Some things will never be released and that is just how it is. Sometimes the real thing to let go of is the expectation that anything ought to be any other way than how it is right now. Sometimes the release is a release of control and a full surrender to what is.

How long will it take to let go?
It's like asking "how long is the correct amount of time to take a poo?"

The answer is — as long as it takes.
We do our best and we let the rest go.

: :

How can I let go

when it was so very bad?

Why would I hold on?

: :

I am full of shit.

How can I know who I am

until I let go?

Unclenching From The World We Have Known

If we are going to experience a healthy future, it's not only personal things we need to let go of, we also need to unclench from the world as we have known it.

The things desired and undesired from our past have moved through us. Just like the clean-eating vegan I referred to earlier, no matter what has happened *around* us or *to* us or *to our ancestors*, we *cannot* move forward without releasing the old self, the old world, the old thinking, the old ideas.

It's a paradox — *learn* from the past, yet *release* the past. Take in all the good nourishment, yet don't hold on to it. It seems impossible but navigating that razor-fine edge is the way to create the most amount of space to receive the new.

There is SO MUCH MORE for us!!

There is more delicious food to eat, more experiences to have, more places to visit, more people to meet, more ideas and solutions, more songs to hear, more stories, more dancing, more inventions, more of LIFE to take in!

It didn't start out as shit.

Just because it's a shitshow now, does not mean it was shit going in. In fact, it could have been nourishing going in, it was fragrant and delicious.

We can't eat all of the food that we will ever eat in our lives right this minute — we munch in pieces, in slices, in morsels, in sips — then we let that move on through to make room for more.

No matter how yummy that food was at first, it will all eventually turn to shit. The fact remains, if we hold on to anything, it becomes toxic. Even spring water will become putrid if it is left to stand without movement.

What I'm saying is not a philosophy, it's not a "belief," it's not a law or rule —it's just literally how all humans, all animals, all of our planets, our galaxies and our Universes work.

It appears to be the only way anything works.

As healthy or desirable as the past may have been
(was it though?) the only way forward is to let it go.
We must choose again
and again
and again
what we will feed on and what we decide we will be
nourished by in each fresh moment.

::

What if I don't like

who I am without it all?

Who will I be then?

::

Honestly, I hope

a new, warm-water bidet

is in my future.

On "Calling Someone Out On Their Shit" *or* "Whoever Smelt It - Dealt It"

Some thoughts about judging

I have a long and deep history with judging others. I was raised on it. And it raised me.

If being judgmental were an Olympic Sport, I would certainly have a few gold medals on my wall by now.

No one has been safe from my judgments — especially myself.

When we judge others, it is energetically loud and most of us can all pick up on it crystal clear. Have you ever felt the judgments of others without them saying a word? It is extremely painful and difficult to ignore once you feel it.

Here's a little way that I comfort myself when I am feeling judged by others. It's how I help myself remember that I don't have to join them in judging me while simultaneously letting them have the experience of the energy they themselves are putting out there.

I imagine judging others is like this...

Visualize soaking in a fresh warm bathtub and you release a turd right there in the water.

That turd is your nugget of judgement.

You are the only one to fully experience all the gross repercussions of putting that shit out there.

For example, if you judge me, I do not have to choose to get in that bathtub with you.

That's all yours.

I'm gonna leave you and your judgments to experience one another.

I still judge though.

I've had plenty of floaty doo-doo baths. I know the rank feeling of being constipated with resentment and backed up with self-righteousness about how I imagine a situation should have gone or what someone should (or should not) have said or done or thought or believed.

When we were kids, if someone farted and someone else made a big deal about it, we would say "whoever smelt it, dealt it." The idea being, if you are calling it out on someone else, it's because you are trying to deflect responsibility and put a little shame out there on others.

It is often the case that when we judge someone else harshly, it's because it is something we judge harshly about ourselves, and we want to shame others before we are discovered. We secretly might believe we are deserving of the shame we were trying to off-load on to someone else.

My self-shame belongs in the toilet along with all the other things that I'm trying to let go of. If I keep it, I get it all over myself and everyone else who tries to get close to me.

Now, there is an argument to be made that judging is a natural thing we do and we ought not judge ourselves for judging. While I can understand their point, I feel like the turd-in-the-tub anal-ogy still holds up.

Here's the way I see it, we don't need to judge ourselves for judging, the same way we don't need to shame ourselves for pooping. It's natural.

The issue is where, when, and how will you deal with your own turd-of-judgment? Are you identifying with that judgment you have of another or of yourself?

Do you really want that thing floating around in your fresh warm tub, or would you rather let that floater move on through and out?

When we freely spout off all the ways that we think others ought to behave or believe we are letting the world know the judgments we actually hold of ourselves.

That turd is in your own tub. Not theirs.

Whoever smelt it, dealt it.

I still judge though, only it feels so much grosser to me now than it used to, and at least that's a start.

: :

It's time to let go.

How easy can I make it

to never return?

: :

Judgments float around

like fresh turds on the water.

Is this what I want?

The Water & The Fire

Rituals you can use to stick the dismount with grace.

The water ritual in two parts

Part 1. Water cleansing is historically used in ritual as a symbol of purification and renewal. Water is also broadly recognized as a symbol for emotions.

The ritual act of the flush seals the deal and guarantees that it's really gone.

Try saying something like "May the water carry away all that I have released and left behind."

And should your release require a mid-scene courtesy-flush, even better!

Part 2. We wash our hands of it in a literal act of removing any residue of our underworld which may have hopped a ride on our fingers. We want to eat and connect in relationships with clean hands now.

We use soap and water to cleanse and purify our hands. It is a useful time to connect to how you wish to proceed when you set foot back into the regular world. Set an intention about what you will focus on now, what you will give your attention to, and what you will create with those clean and creative hands.

The fire

Light that match, friend, and do a nice thing for yourself and any innocent by-standers.

The use of fire in ritual is as old as time. The element of fire has a purifying and transformational impact on everything that it touches. Nothing is ever the same again after it comes in contact with fire.

When the air is thick with the reality of all that has just been released, it takes a simple strike of a match to miraculously transform the very air you breathe.

Light a match then put it right out. It completely shifts the mood in the air.

A physical reminder that the old is gone, consumed by the alchemical fires of digestion. The cleansing element of water takes it away and the sulfuric spark of a match finishes the job.

Water, fire, and intention work together. These are tools to support letting go the whole way. This creates space for new experiences, new nourishments, new life for us to digest and create from.

It feels good to leave the room and all of the past behind.

Take in a fresh, clean breath on the other side of the door.

It is done.

: :

Water is Holy.

Element of our cleansing.

Everyday Magic.

: :

I remember now

all the different ways that I

can let the past go.

The "To DooDoo List"

Start a private "to doodoo" note on your phone (oh - please remember to make it private!). Throughout your day, make bullet points of things you notice *when* you notice them.

Anytime you catch a whiff of a sticky, ruminating thought, jot it down.

Perhaps you just realized that something which was once desirable, has turned toxic. Make a quick note of it.

In fact, the simple act of jotting it down in your private document is the beginning of letting it go.

You can reference this list any time you need a reminder of the things you are dropping.

Whereas the "Analog Poo" session is when you leave your phone behind; if you find that is with you, referencing the "to doodoo list" is a great way to keep focus on the task at hand rather than doom scrolling.

Imagine you are sitting down on the crapper, "under the gun", crowning with urgency; and for the life of you, you cannot remember all the emotional things you want to let go of in that hot second. You're busy.

Your list will help you make the most of what you make.

Once you have picked one item from the list, your cells and synapses are now paying attention. Your body knows what to do.

And when you have done the deed, wipe that line from your note.

As if it never existed.

Remember, these notes are *not* for record keeping.

They are for action taking.

PRO TIP: Trust Yourself. This is *your* practice. I playfully offer these ideas to deepen your inner work. But really, any way to make this practice your own, will always yield the truest, most desirable outcome.

Ready To Experiment?

Here are some steps to try

1. Assign meaning to this particular poo. Make it short and sweet and something you are seriously exhausted of replaying or remembering. Consult your "To DooDoo List" if nothing immediately comes to mind.

2. Imagine that all of your cells understand the assignment and are carrying away whatever you told your mind and heart to release.

3. Do the doodoo.

4. Say something like this to yourself.
   (Note: this part is not an affirmation, that comes later. This is the verbal act of getting that shit out.)
   "I declare that I will not bring this turd back up casually in conversation.

   I will not review the ways I was wronged and re-injure myself in the process.

I will not re-play what I should have said
instead.

I will not turn on myself as a punishment for
being a regular human."

5. Flush it.
6. Wash your hands. Let the water feel good.
7. Feed on some nourishing thoughts like these...
   "I believe the best about myself and my
   intentions."

   "I remember that the things others do is a
   reflection of themselves and their own
   mental/emotional state — not mine."

   "I remember that I am not my thoughts."

   "Regardless of my circumstances, my value
   remains."

"I choose my thoughts, my actions and my perspective."

"I create loving thoughts about myself in the past, myself now, and myself in the future."

"I enthusiastically imagine an outcome that I truly desire!"

Let's put it all together

Here is an example, you could say something like this:

Dear body,
I want to finally be done feeling embarrassed about that
thing I said in front of all those people. I want to stop
replaying it in my head now.

I have decided that I will not bring this turd back up
casually in conversation. I will not re-play what I should
have said instead. I will not be mean to myself about this
subject anymore.

Those thoughts will be gone the way this poop will
be over and forgotten forever. I am deciding this
now.

If I need more help to release, I will ask for professional
support.
It is healthy for me to let this go now.

I love myself and I trust that I am always growing and changing. I am making room for new experiences, new conversations, new people in my life.

I shift the energy of my thoughts now.
I release the past and set my foot on the path I wish to take.

Yours Forever,
Me

In case of emergency

Have a plan for what to do if/when the pipes get clogged with an especially sticky thought that you recently flushed. Should that thought-turd float back up in your mind make this declaration to yourself

"I don't *think* about that shit anymore"
or
"I don't *talk* about that shit anymore."

and then immediately change the subject in your head.

Have a good thought locked and loaded to fill in the vacancy you just created. You can even make a cheat sheet for yourself in your notes app as a safety measure so you don't have to come up with a more nourishing thought to think on the spot.

It could go something like this:

> *"I don't think about*
> *that shit anymore, I*
> *love myself and I trust*
> *my instincts."*

then move on swiftly and get out of that shitstorm of gross thoughts. Acknowledge, course-correct, then move on. It can be a 10 second shift.

Make Peace With The Release

A peaceful world is not simply a world without military war. A peaceful world is made up of peaceful people in it.

For instance, have you ever been in a super chill environment with people who know you and love you yet, yet, on the inside, there is a wild, violent war erupting? Your mind whips up all these certainties about the ill intentions of others, and your brain is crafting the perfect accusations. Critical, angry thoughts are whipping around like an army of flying monkeys ready to strike making it impossible to enjoy yourself?

Have you ever done this?

I have.

Or, on the other hand, have you ever been in a room where everyone was all punchy and combative, but for some reason you just didn't feel the same way as them?

Have you ever had the experience of being in your own personal bubble of good juice regardless of the way the people around you are behaving?

I have too.

Your peace and mine does not come from a peaceful environment (although that helps). It has a lot more to do with how much shit you are carrying around with you into the world.

Each one of us is in charge of our own peace. It will not come from the outside. It comes from the inside job of releasing any attachment to the past — not because the past was bad (though it may have been). We let go because those are the mechanics of our material world. I didn't make this up; I'm just observing what is so.

No matter how much war there is, inner peace comes from the inner release.

Peace comes from unclenching from the grip of thinking we need to control circumstances in life and instead surrender to the physics of it all. It's a big ask, and since we may not know how to mentally unclench, we can count on the built-in forces of nature that exist to work on your behalf and let the body do the heavy lifting.

We are creatures in a system with reliable gravity, digestive chemistry, cells being born, cells dying, and involuntary muscle contractions. All of these forces of nature are fully designed to make for the easiest, most efficient exit strategy.

This is GOOD NEWS!! You are not an exception to physics, or chemistry, or gravity! Your peace will never come from the outside world conforming to your will. Peace is a thing that can happen regardless of circumstance.

Our minds make it tricky to let go of the past, but our bodies are hard-wired for it.

Imagine if you had to mentally sort out the nutrients from the waste? If we had to do calculations in chemistry and engineering just to get the things we need from our food, we'd all starve to death!

Peace is resting in the knowledge that you are not personally in charge of everything that happens in the world or even in your own body. Some things just happen and they don't need to be judged or shamed or blamed.

: :

We did not speak much

in this book of gas or farts.

'Twas too on the nose.

: :

If I could have found

a less-gross way to say this,

maybe I would have.

A Little Confession

There is much more that I could say to expand on this evergreen *anal*-ogy, but I think you get the idea.

So now I'm gonna come clean.

I didn't write this little book *just* so that you can have more useful poops, although I hope that you do.

This book is actually the first part of an elaborate *love*-scheme on my part.

I wrote this book so that you might have room enough to receive the good stuff that life is offering you.

While I'm excited about what I am creating next, there are *new* ideas, *new* solutions, *new* paths, and *new* ways of thinking that are emerging all over the world right now! There are answers everywhere coming through ordinary people – and that includes YOU!

The catch is, in order to let in the good stuff that you are designed to experience, you will *definitely* need to know how to leave some bull shit behind. Fortunately, we've already begun the process with this book.

And now that we have made room for what we actually prefer, we can create future experiences of our *truest desires.*

A Consensual Blessing

I want to share my BeautifulFuture Blessing with you. I speak it over myself regularly, and it is the pivot point around which my life and all of my work revolves.

I mean every word deeply and sincerely and I hope that you receive it in that spirit. It is a morsel of nourishment for you after such a brave experience of release if you desire it.

However, in my experience, *non-consensual* blessings are rather ineffective and mostly fluff. Therefore, with your consent, I ask you to read it and *mean* it for yourself.

Then after you read The BeautifulFuture Blessing, I invite you to reflect on your own body wisdom.

Notice how it feels inside. Do you feel any tingles? Sparkles? A flutter in your gut? Happy little watery eyes? Any physical sensations as you read it?

If you have a pleasant feeling reading it, this could mean that the blessing has nourishment for you. When something feels like a "yes" to us it is *sensational*. We get a body sensation, a somatic body- knowing washes over us, and we may notice that our nervous systems begin to settle.

If you don't have any feeling in your body at all there is still nourishment in it for you if you want it.

One way to let in the good juice of this blessing is you might put one hand on your belly and one hand on your heart as you say the blessing out loud to yourself.

You can change the word "You" to the word "I."
Say the blessing out loud and bless your own self.

The most potent and effective kind of blessing is the one you offer to yourself.

If you are ready?

I invite you

to take...

four...

deep...

breaths...

then turn the page.

The BeautifulFuture Blessing

May you create anew according to your Pleasure
May you shine your glorious Light
May you take Mature, Responsible Care
of your creations
May you know that you are Safe
and
May you honor the truth and fullness of your being
in your experience of
Pleasure
Beauty
Renewal
&
Devotion.
So I say, and So it Is.

Check in with yourself now...

What did you notice?

What do you wonder?

What do you feel?

Whatever you received is nourishment for YOU from YOU.

You can come back to this blessing whenever you like and juice up on your own good vibes.

It's Time To "Go"

Well, Friend,

I hope you got what you came for, and more than you could have imagined.

I know I did!

Writing this book has been a total thrill and a STEEP learning curve! It is only now that it's complete that I finally get the punchline of the joke I set up for myself all those years ago.

While I believe many people will benefit greatly from this book, the person who most needed this message right now was me. Turns out this book is my own elaborate love-scheme to get *me* to be brave enough to let in *my* own good!

The fact that you are holding my first book in your hands is material proof that this *shit really works*! At least it does for me. I really hope it works for you too, friend.

Look at us! You and I here, together at the threshold of transformation, cracking poop jokes and laughing all the way to The BeautifulFuture.

How easy can we make this?
How much better can we make it feel?

Rather Boldly,
Kimberly

Bonus Drop

Write your own HaiPoo

Sharing what works for me in case it works for you, too.

I find writing haiku to be a great way for me to distill a lot of complex ideas and feelings into a bite-sized morsel. I can be with big feelings more easily when I make myself have to say it in three little lines.

Here's how it works
: :

A haiku is a poem of three lines

Line One has 5 syllables

Line two has 7 syllables

Line Three has 5 syllables

And if writing a HaiPoo isn't your jam, by all means, use this space to write or draw anything that inspires you to let go and make a fresh start

_____

_____

_____

_____

_____

_____

_____

_____

_____

Great-Fullness and Thanks

to the people who have been on this first book
journey with me.
To the neighborhood friends who listened to me read
parts of it out loud through giggles and snorts over the
years, to the kind ones who read my shitty first drafts
and who encouraged me to keep going, to the brave
beloveds willing to tell me where they felt lost and who
challenged me to be clearer and bring more of myself
out.

Thank you. I love you.

Tim Clo, Zoraida Ojeda, Ray Pelletier, Kenny Clo, Aslan Clo,

Cristarelli Berber, Miles Frizzell, Shannon Jackson Arnold,

Cynthia Hudson, Marnie Kate Hudson, Katherine Petillo,

Thomas Orr Anderson, Michelle Gannon, nic strack,

Leigh Anne Strictland, Chris Dauphin, Elizabeth Cook,

Fairlight Hubbard, Marcy Kalinowski, Margaret Littman

James-Olivia Chu Hillman, and Amanda O'Brien.

And from the tenderest part of my heart,

I bow in deep gratitude to

Mack Page and Amanda Page

whose life-force, encouragement and delight is what gave

me the courage to create this book in the first place.

About The Author

Kimberly Clo is a Nashville-based visual artist, teacher and author. This is her debut title.

She creates futuristic, geometric art that was born of her contemplative practice of Sacred Geometry.

Kimberly's art, along with her passionate and fiery way of communicating, *ignites* creativity, *illuminates* self-discovery and *inspires* transformation in her students.

After people encounter Kimberly, they often experience fresh insights and new perspectives about themselves and the world.

They leave with a new hope and enthusiasm to create their own version of BeautifulFuture in the BeautifulRightNow.

Known for the beloved :: EMBRACE :: mural in the heart of downtown Nashville, Kimberly's art elevates consciousness everywhere it goes — from corporate offices and private homes to healing spaces and public installations. Infusing spaces with futuristic inspiration and soulful, heart-centered connection, initiating powerful transformative experiences.

Visit my website and join my email list
so we can stay connected
in The BeautifulFuture

www.KimberlyClo.com

All that can shake will shake.
All that cannot shake will remain.
I remain.

www.ingramcontent.com/pod-product-compliance
Lightning Source LLC
Chambersburg PA
CBHW020755130626
46554CB00006B/2206